NAME

DATE

ABOUT THE

Pour Out Your Heart

PRAYER JOURNAL

This journal is a tool to help you develop a lifelong pattern of gospel-centered, Scripture-based prayer. It is not something you will complete in a week or even a year. But over time, this little book will grow into a valuable treasure, a safe place to pour out your heart before the Lord, and an ever-deepening reminder of his promises and faithfulness to you. To begin, turn the page and follow the step-by-step introduction.

HOW TO USE THIS JOURNAL

A STEP-BY-STEP INTRODUCTION

By following these seven steps, you'll learn to how to set up and use this journal. Each section is designed to help you develop a different area of your prayer life. Remember, using this journal is meant to be a way to unburden your heart, not add a burdensome duty. Feel free to go at your own pace.

(1) **Get acquainted.** Simply spend some time getting familiar with the the basic structure of the sections and the heart behind them. Begin by flipping through every page. Then read the first two articles in Section 5 entitled "The Story Behind This Journal" and "What Is Prayer?"

(2) **Start in the Daily Gospel Truth section.** Read the instructions on page 10. Then start by simply writing out and praying through one verse that has helped you know the redeeming love of Christ.

(3) **Add a verse to the Promises section.** Read the instructions on page 28. Then start by writing and praying through one verse that has ministered to you. For a list of suggested verses refer to page 207.

(4) **Begin to use the Kingdom Prayers section.** Read the instructions on page 57. Write one verse to pray for unbelievers on page 209.

(5) **Setup the Prayers for Loved Ones section.** Read the instructions on page 73. Begin by adding the names of those closest to you to the top of the first few pages. Then add a verse and pray it for one person.

(6) **Write a prayer in the Prayers for Myself section.** Read the instructions on page 137. Find a meaningful borrowed prayer on page 217 to write out on the first pages.

(7) **Setup the Provisions section.** Read the instructions on page 180 and decide on a regular cadence for reflecting on and recording God's big provisions to you and your family. Start by adding a verse to page 181.

With that, you've completed the introduction! As you've seen, each section has its own cadence and rhythm. You'll visit some sections frequently and some you may only visit once or twice a year or as the need arises. For more on suggested rhythms and uses see the article in Resources entitled "A Final Word of Encouragement."

Pour Out Your Heart Prayer Journal: A Planner for a Life of Prayer

Copyright © 2022 by Lois Krogh

Published by Crossway
1300 Crescent Street
Wheaton, Illinois 60187

Cover Design: Dana Tanamachi

Artwork: Dana Tanamachi

First printing 2022

Printed in China

Cloth over Board ISBN: 978-1-4335-7976-9

Crossway is a publishing ministry of Good News Publishers

RRDS   29   28   27   26   25   24   23   22
10   9   8   7   6   5   4   3   2   1

SECTIONS

Believers do not pray with the view of informing God about things unknown to Him, or of exciting Him to do His duty, or of urging Him as though He were reluctant. On the contrary, they pray in order that they may arouse to seek Him, that they may exercise their faith in meditating on His promises, that they may relieve themselves from their anxieties by pouring them into His bosom; in a word, that they may declare that from Him alone they hope and expect, both for themselves and for others, all good things.

JOHN CALVIN

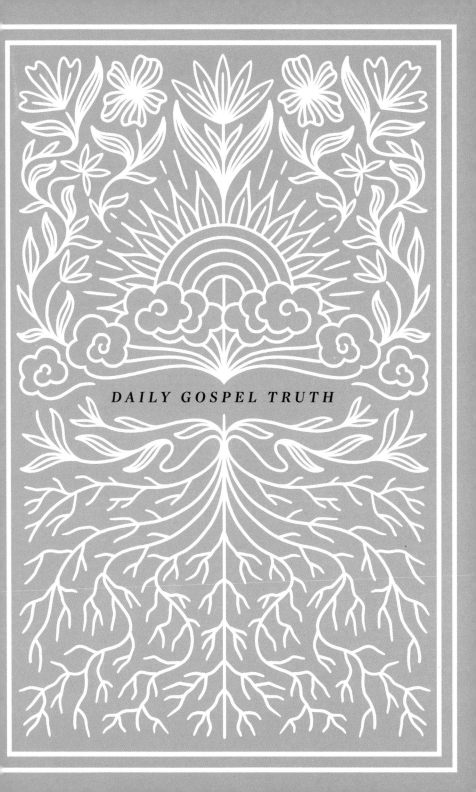

DAILY GOSPEL TRUTH

DAILY GOSPEL TRUTH

Because of our tendency to slip so quickly into legalism, to expect that our actions earn us God's favor or disapproval, and to walk in the pride of doing things "right," we need to breathe in gospel truth daily. We come confidently to God in prayer because of Christ's righteousness, not our own. Daily gospel truth reminds us of this.

Have you heard the exhortation to "preach the gospel to yourself every day"? What does this mean exactly? Paul Tripp explains that preaching the gospel to ourselves involves "self-consciously and intentionally reminding ourselves of the person and presence and provisions of our Redeemer."[1] The gospel is not only good news regarding our salvation; it is good news about our growth in Christlikeness.

The first pages of this journal, Daily Gospel Truth, are the place to begin your time in prayer with a reminder of God's grace and mercy.

Fill out these pages by

1. writing out verses that proclaim the gospel (p. 11)
2. writing out hymn lyrics, catechism questions and answers, or meaningful quotes (p. 16)
3. writing out the gospel message in your own words (p. 22)

1 Paul Tripp, "Preach the Gospel to Yourself," *Desiring God*, April 5, 2014, https://www.desiringgod.org/interviews/preach-the-gospel-to-yourself/.

Bless the Lord, O my soul,
and forget not all his benefits,

PSALM 103:2

In Your Own Words

Write out the gospel in your own words. What you write does not have to be a perfect and complete theological statement. As you grow in your understanding of God's Word, you can go back and rework this section as needed. (For an example of the gospel written in your own words, see page 211.)

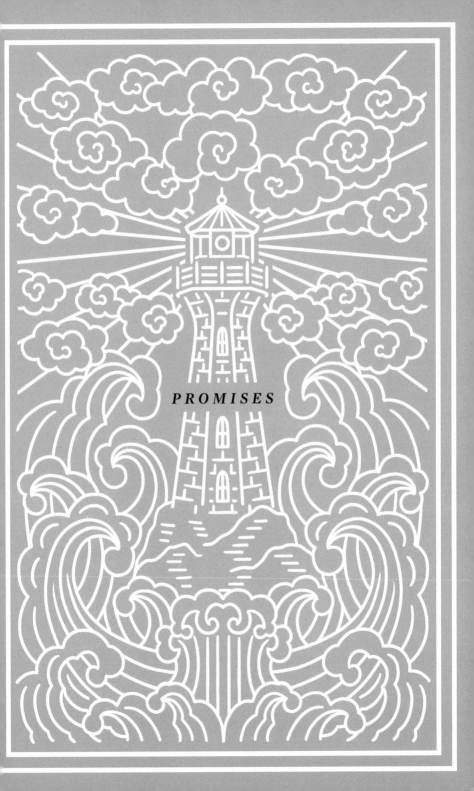

PROMISES

PROMISES

According to archaeologists, the steps leading to the Jerusalem temple were constructed in such a way that a person had to slow down in order to climb them. We too need to slow down as we walk into God's presence. Meditating on the promises of God helps us do so.

God is a promise-making, promise-keeping God. He delights to have his children call on him to keep his promises. Starting with the promises of God helps us to know what to ask God for when we pray. Reciting the promises of God also strengthens us to come boldly into his presence.

Are there verses that are "your promises"? Verses that have ministered peace and grace and truth to you in a specific situation? These are the types of verses to write out in this section. See page 207 for a list of suggested Scripture promises. As you spend time in the Word, you will find additional verses to include as well.

Life is often messy and unsettling. Use times of disquiet to search the Scriptures for verses that speak truth to the moment. Write them in this section.

Every word of God proves true;
he is a shield to those who take refuge in him.
PROVERBS 30:5

Has he said, and will he not do it?
Or has he spoken, and will he not fulfill it?
NUMBERS 23:19b

PRAYERS

PRAYERS

The Bible assures us that God hears and answers our prayers. Hebrews 4:16 reminds us that we can come confidently to the throne of grace:

> Let us then with confidence draw near to the throne of grace, that we may receive mercy and find grace to help in time of need.

Prayer is the heart of this journal. We will divide our prayers into three major categories: Kingdom Prayers (p. 57), Prayers for Loved Ones (p. 73), and Prayers for Myself (p. 137).

A Note about Sticky Notes

As we begin this section, you may find yourself wondering how it will be possible to record so many prayers in a journal intended for use over a long period of time. The answer is sticky notes!

Using sticky notes in your journal will enable you to continue to use it for many years. You can use them in a couple ways. The first is for prayers for groups of people. (You will learn who these groups are as you get to each section.) Write the name of groups you are praying for on sticky notes and place the sticky notes on the left side of the page. On the opposite page and those following it, write out several beloved Scripture passages.

When praying for an individual person, enduring truths and "big-picture Scripture prayers" (verses you intend to pray over that person for many years) are written directly on the appropriate pages in the journal. Specific, time-sensitive, subject-to-change prayer requests are written on sticky notes and placed in the journal.

Prayer requests written on sticky notes will include prayers about things such as making a friend, choosing a school, finding a spouse, changing jobs, or accomplishing specific ministry goals. Some of these requests are more date specific: a test, a quarrel that needs resolving, a financial need. Sticky notes can be easily switched out and revised.

Use the blank space provided on the first page of each section to hold your sticky notes. By using the notes in this way, your journal will never have "old" prayer requests in it. It will remain current and yet timeless.

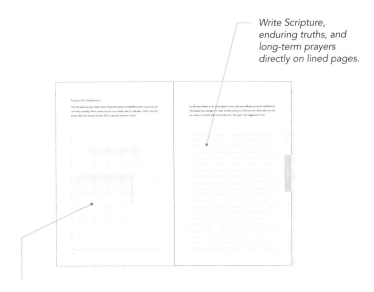

Write Scripture, enduring truths, and long-term prayers directly on lined pages.

Place sticky notes on left side containing groups of people or specific, time-sensitive prayer requests.

. . . and call upon me in the day of trouble;
I will deliver you, and you shall glorify me.

PSALM 50:15

I love the Lord, because he has heard
my voice and my pleas for mercy.
Because he inclined his ear to me,
therefore I will call on him as long as I live.

PSALM 116:1–2

He will not let your foot be moved;
he who keeps you will not slumber.

PSALM 121:3

"Ask, and it will be given to you; seek, and you will find; knock, and it will be opened to you. . . . If you then, who are evil, know how to give good gifts to your children, how much more will your Father who is in heaven give good things to those who ask him!"

MATTHEW 7:7, 11

Likewise the Spirit helps us in our weakness. For we do not know what to pray for as we ought, but the Spirit himself intercedes for us with groanings too deep for words.

ROMANS 8:26

Now to him who is able to do far more abundantly than all that we ask or think, according to the power at work within us, to him be glory in the church and in Christ Jesus throughout all generations, forever and ever. Amen.

EPHESIANS 3:20–21

PART 1

Kingdom Prayers

The Lord's Prayer begins with an upward focus— we are to ask that God's name be honored, that his kingdom be established, and that his will become the joyful endeavor of all people. We will use three subcategories under Kingdom Prayers: Prayers for Unbelievers, Prayers for the Household of Faith, and Prayers for the Advancement of Christ's Kingdom.

Prayers for Unbelievers

Use this space to post sticky notes listing the names of unbelievers for whom you are currently praying. Some names may be on a sticky note for decades. Others may be people that God has put in your life at a precise moment in time.

On the lines below, write out Scripture verses that you will use to pray for unbelievers. The names may change over time, but the verses you will pray over those who have not yet come to the faith will remain the same. See page 209 for suggested verses.

Prayers for the Household of Faith

Use this space to post sticky notes listing the names of believers with or for whom you minister and for whom you are praying. The sticky notes in this section might hold the names of people in your small group, people you are discipling, or your church's pastors and leaders.

On the lines below, write out Scripture verses to use when praying for believers. Consider using the prayers Paul includes in his letters to churches. See page 210 for other suggested verses.

Prayers for the Advancement of Christ's Kingdom

Use this space to post sticky notes listing the names of missionaries and ministries for whom you pray.

On the lines below, write out Scriptures related to gospel proclamation. See page 210 for suggested verses.

PART 2

Prayers for Loved Ones

This is the section of our journal where you will pray for your family and friends—those dearest to you. Each page is highly customizable. There are two general ways you can use them. Either write a group of people at the top (like Extended Family or Work Associates) and add sticky notes with names and prayer requests, or write the name of an individual (like your husband or daughter) and use sticky notes to capture time-sensitive prayer requests for that person. In both cases, use the right side and subsequent pages to record Scripture and long-term prayers.

Use this space to post sticky notes with time-sensitive prayer requests. For groups, add multiple sticky notes with individual names.

On the lines below, write out Scripture verses and long-term prayers. See page 210 for suggested verses and page 213 for sample prayers based on Scripture.

Use this space to post sticky notes with time-sensitive prayer requests. For groups, add multiple sticky notes with individual names.

On the lines below, write out Scripture verses and long-term prayers. See page 210 for
suggested verses and page 213 for sample prayers based on Scripture.

Use this space to post sticky notes with time-sensitive prayer requests. For groups, add multiple sticky notes with individual names.

On the lines below, write out Scripture verses and long-term prayers. See page 210 for suggested verses and page 213 for sample prayers based on Scripture.

Use this space to post sticky notes with time-sensitive prayer requests. For groups, add multiple sticky notes with individual names.

On the lines below, write out Scripture verses and long-term prayers. See page 210 for suggested verses and page 213 for sample prayers based on Scripture.

Use this space to post sticky notes with time-sensitive prayer requests. For groups, add multiple sticky notes with individual names.

On the lines below, write out Scripture verses and long-term prayers. See page 210 for suggested verses and page 213 for sample prayers based on Scripture.

Use this space to post sticky notes with time-sensitive prayer requests. For groups, add multiple sticky notes with individual names.

On the lines below, write out Scripture verses and long-term prayers. See page 210 for suggested verses and page 213 for sample prayers based on Scripture.

Use this space to post sticky notes with time-sensitive prayer requests. For groups, add multiple sticky notes with individual names.

On the lines below, write out Scripture verses and long-term prayers. See page 210 for suggested verses and page 213 for sample prayers based on Scripture.

Use this space to post sticky notes with time-sensitive prayer requests. For groups, add multiple sticky notes with individual names.

On the lines below, write out Scripture verses and long-term prayers. See page 210 for suggested verses and page 213 for sample prayers based on Scripture.

Prayers for Myself

This section will become very personal and unique to you. For example, you could write your life verse. Or you could record prayers you come across that prove meaningful to you. Or you could write down prayers of repentance and cries for help regarding any pattern of sin in your life. If a book you read or a sermon you hear touches your heart, write out what you want to remember in the form of a prayer. As in previous sections, you'll use the left side of the first page for sticky notes with specific or time-sensitive prayer requests.

Prayers for Myself

Use this space to post sticky notes with specific, time-sensitive prayer requests.

On the lines below, write out Scripture verses, borrowed prayers, Bible study notes, or simply pour your heart out before the Lord.

PROVISIONS

PROVISIONS

It is good to record God's work in our lives and how he has answered our prayers. Doing so is a great way to look back over a year and be thankful. Rather than listing every daily grace, consider writing out five to eight significant ways in which you and your family have seen the Lord's hand direct your lives in the past year.

When you are beginning your journal, you may want to spend a longer time going back through the years and recording the highlights of God's provision up to this point. Going forward you may consider doing this at the end of each year between Christmas and the New Year.

Come and hear, all you who fear God,
and I will tell what he has done for my soul.

PSALM 66:16

I will remember the deeds of the LORD;
yes, I will remember your wonders of old.

PSALM 77:11

One generation shall commend your works to another,
and shall declare your mighty acts.

PSALM 145:4

O LORD, you are my God;
I will exalt you; I will praise your name,
for you have done wonderful things,
plans formed of old, faithful and sure.

ISAIAH 25:1

Verses

Use this first page to record Scripture verses about God's provision for his people. Then use the next pages to record those provisions over the years.

DATE:

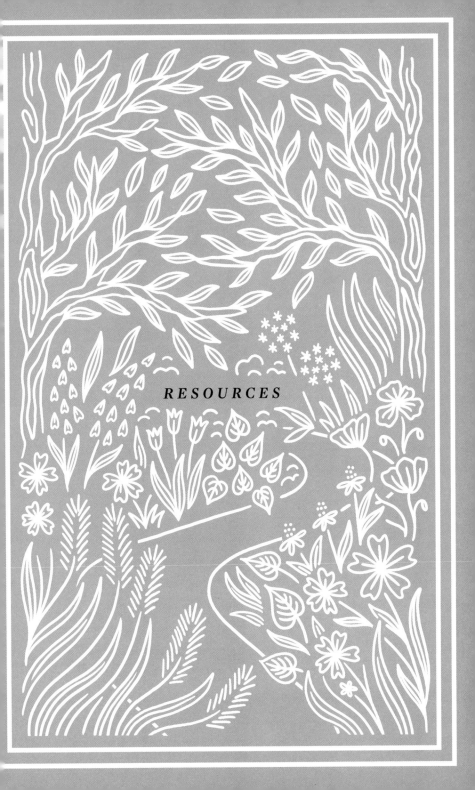

RESOURCES

THE STORY BEHIND
THIS JOURNAL

During a time of personal reflection at a women's retreat in 2000, I read Psalm 62:8 and Proverbs 30:5:

> Trust in him at all times, O people;
> > pour out your heart before him;
> > God is a refuge for us.

> Every word of God proves true;
> > he is a shield to those who take refuge in him.

I needed a refuge. I was a pastor's wife in a new community, homeschooling five children and caring for my elderly parents.

That day, my prayer journal began to take shape. It became a simple way to pour out my heart to the Lord and remind myself of his promises. For twenty years it has aided me in being more consistent, biblical, and intentional in praying for my family and friends. It has helped me think about things from a kingdom perspective. It has broken my self-sufficiency and made me welcome weakness. It has taken my eyes off my worries and compelled me to look expectantly to Jesus.

Though it is a difficult thing to admit, especially for seasoned believers, many of us struggle to pray. A key purpose of this journal and this system is to transform and strengthen your prayer life by helping you to pray the Scriptures. Prayer that is not Scripture infused can become sentimental, overly focused on ourselves and on temporal issues. The ancient Christian practice of praying Scripture can strengthen our hope and deepen our faith. Simply put, praying Scripture teaches us what to pray for.

The focus of this journal is prayer for the people God has brought into your life. Praying for others reduces my anxiety about them as I cast my cares on the One who cares for me. By praying specific verses for the people in my life, I begin to think about their lives in view of God's kingdom purposes, and my love for those individuals increases.

This prayer journal is one person's system. It is not inspired Scripture nor a guarantee of a pain-free, struggle-free life. This is not "the *right* way to pray." It is a tool.

Your journal is not a project you will finish in an afternoon, nor a "fill-it-up-and-it's-done" project. The usefulness and value of your journal will develop over time as you personalize it and use it. Doing so will take time, even years.

I pray that as you use your journal, continuing to add to it for years to come, God will perform a beautiful work of grace in your life.

Lois Krogh

WHAT IS PRAYER?

Pouring out one's heart in prayer to God is a lifelong practice that results in life-giving blessings, the best of which are a deeper awareness of the heart of God and the experience of a soul at rest.

Too often we make prayer simply an item to check off our to-do list. Sometimes what we call prayer is, in reality, merely thoughts about how difficult our lives are or daydreams about how our circumstances need to change.

Neither of these mindsets is correct. How, then, should we define prayer and capture its true purpose and meaning? *Prayer is connecting with God. It is the pouring out of your heart to a loving heavenly Father, aware that he hears you.*

Psalm 62 is an example of prayer.

A common heading given to this psalm is "My Soul Waits for God Alone." This comes from three uses of the word "alone" in vv. 1, 2, 5 and the use of the word "only" in verse 6. "For God alone my soul waits" (v. 1). "He alone is my rock and my salvation" (v. 2).

God's help is unequalled and unrivaled. No one else—*nothing else*—can be my rock, my salvation, my fortress, my hope, my refuge. He alone is my strength and my safety.

In verses 11 and 12 the psalmist tells us that power and steadfast love belong to God. This is who he is. No one else is power. No one else is steadfast love.

Why does the psalmist need strength and safety? The reasons are plentiful. Deceitful people are trying to ruin him (vv. 3, 4). Life is short, men cannot be trusted, and riches do not bring security (vv. 9, 10).

The stanzas of this psalm go back and forth between the "only-ness" of God and the desperate straits of the psalmist. In verse 8 the psalmist turns to give instruction to his listeners:

Trust in him at all times, O people;
    pour out your heart before him;
    God is a refuge for us.

Trust in God — because he is the only one who can be trusted.
Pour out your heart — with complete honesty and total open-
        ness, give voice to all your desires and dreams.
Before him — in God's presence, in prayer.

This is prayer. Praying is not a burdensome task. It is an unbur-dening of the heart.

Whether my heart is heavily weighed down or bubbling with joy, when it is dark with doubt and fear or perplexed by the unknown, I come to him who alone is my strength and refuge, and I tell him everything.

What Are the Prerequisites for Prayer?

Prayer is not only for people who have been Christians for a long time. Our first cry to God, "Lord have mercy," continues to be a great example of prayer. Put away any thought of needing to be perfect. Perfection is never a prerequisite to prayer.

Humility, however, is.

Prayer cannot begin with the prideful belief that, if I pray, God must fix things. Prayer is not a duty we perform in exchange for good things from God. Nor should it be a crisis-inspired demand for what we have decided we deserve. Such misunderstandings put God and us on the same level as equals in a business exchange. Or worse—they imagine God as our servant.

Like Job, we need to see God as he truly is, as sovereign over us, and humble ourselves. To paraphrase Job, we must say, "I will not demand that I understand things that are too wonderful for me to know" (see Job 42:3). For "God opposes the proud but gives grace to the humble" (1 Pet. 5:5).

She who would pour out her heart to the Lord needs a Mary-like attitude of humility: "Behold, I am the servant of the Lord; let it be to me according to your word" (Luke 1:38).

Another prerequisite to prayer is the recognition of our utter dependence on the Lord. Self-sufficient people don't pray. Why would they need to? Thankfully, God loves his children too much to let us continue in the dangerous lie of self-sufficiency. He puts us in situations beyond our control. And, suddenly, prayer is a necessity. Praying begins in earnest when we admit our neediness, our lack of resources, and our inability to solve problems and fix things.

She who would pour out her heart to the Lord needs a psalmist-like realization of dependence:

As the eyes of a maidservant
    to the hand of her mistress,
so our eyes look to the LORD our God,
    till he has mercy upon us. (Ps. 123:2)

What Happens When We Pray?

There is a great deal that can be said about the relationship between God's sovereign plan and how our prayers are a part of that. We know that for God to be God, he must never change. Our prayers therefore do not change God. And yet, amazingly and mysteriously, God both gives us the desire to pray and uses our prayers to accomplish his will.

God is not waiting for us to explain to him what is happening in our lives. He knows our needs, and he is committed to meeting them (Matt. 6:25–34). "Fear not, little flock, for it is your Father's good pleasure to give you the kingdom" (Luke 12:32).

But God has called us to pray, so that *we* know both our needs and his sufficiency. He is Creator, Sustainer, Savior, and King. He is wise and loving and just, full of grace and truth. He is the one who decrees what is to pass and establishes the steps of our lives. Only he can change the hearts and minds of those we love and direct the outcomes of their lives. When we pray, God lifts the burdens of our hearts onto his back.

And so we pray. We come dependent, submissive, and expectant. We pour out our hearts to the Lord, and we find we are welcomed into his presence with grace and peace.

We pray. God answers. We are helped. He is glorified.

Call upon me in the day of trouble;
> I will deliver you, and you shall glorify me. (Ps. 50:15)

Lois Krogh

SUGGESTED VERSES

Section 1: Daily Gospel Truth

Psalm 103:2	Romans 4:7–8	Colossians 1:13–14,
Isaiah 43:25	Romans 5:8	19–22
Isaiah 53:6	Romans 8:1	Colossians 2:13
John 3:16–17	2 Corinthians 5:21	1 Peter 2:24–25

Section 2: Promises

To Bless Our Trust in Him

Numbers 23:19	Luke 1:45	Romans 3:4

To Carry Our Burdens

Deuteronomy 33:12	Psalm 68:19	1 Peter 5:7
Psalm 50:15	Isaiah 46:3–4	
Psalm 55:22	Matthew 11:28–30	

To Give Us Strength

Psalm 28:8–9	Isaiah 40:31	2 Corinthians 12:9
Psalm 29:10–11	Isaiah 41:10	Ephesians 6:10
Psalm 46:1	Isaiah 45:24	Philippians 4:13

To Safeguard His Church

Isaiah 62:4	Zephaniah 3:15–20	Ephesians 1:22–23
Jeremiah 32:38–41	Matthew 16:18	Ephesians 3:17–19
Ezekiel 34:15–16	John 10:27–28	Ephesians 5:25–27

To Be with Us

Exodus 19:4	Psalm 56:8–9	Zechariah 13:9
Exodus 33:14	Psalm 145:18	Matthew 18:20
Deuteronomy	Psalm 147:11	Matthew 28:20
33:26–27	Isaiah 41:10	Revelation 21:3
Psalm 35:27	Isaiah 54:10	
Psalm 43:3–4	Ezekiel 37:27	

To Comfort Us in Death

Psalm 5:7	Isaiah 25:6–9	Revelation 2:10
Psalm 17:15	1 Corinthians	Revelation 14:13
Psalm 49:15	15:26, 54	Revelation 21:4
Psalm 116:15	Philippians 1:21–23	

To Provide for Us

Psalm 23:1	Psalm 145:15–19	Romans 8:30–31
Psalm 34:8–10	Jeremiah 31:25	2 Corinthian 9:8
Psalm 40:17	Matthew 6:8, 32	Philippians 4:19
Psalm 69:13	Luke 12:32	Hebrews 4:16
Psalm 84:11	John 6:35	

To Reward and Vindicate Us

Genesis 15:1	Deuteronomy 32:4	Psalm 10:14
Genesis 18:25	Ruth 2:12	Psalm 17:2, 7

Psalm 34:15	Isaiah 49:4	Colossians 3:23–24
Psalm 75:2–5	John 1:5	Hebrews 6:10
Psalm 126:5–6	1 Corinthians 4:5	Hebrews 11:6
Psalm 135:14	1 Corinthians 15:58	
Ecclesiastes 12:14	Galatians 6:7–9	

To Fulfill His Purposes for Us

Psalm 31:19	Psalm 138:8	Hosea 6:3
Psalm 32:8	Proverbs 4:18	Philippians 1:6
Psalm 37:4–5	Jeremiah 29:11	1 Thessalonians 5:23

To Calm Our Fears and Give Us Peace

Exodus 14:13–14	Psalm 103:11, 13	John 16:33
Joshua 1:9	Psalm 147:11	Philippians 4:4–7
2 Chronicles 20:5–15	Isaiah 3:10	2 Thessalonians 3:16
Psalm 3:3–6	Isaiah 26:3–4	1 John 4:4
Psalm 33:18–22	Isaiah 43:1	
Psalm 34:7, 9	Isaiah 54:10	

To Give Us Joy

Psalm 4:7	Psalm 16:11
Psalm 5:11	Jeremiah 31:13–14

Section 3: Prayers

For Unbelievers

Daniel 4:34–37	Acts 26:18	2 Corinthians 4:3–6
Psalm 83:18	Romans 2:4	Colossians 1:13
Habakkuk 3:2	1 Corinthians 14:25	1 Thessalonians 2:12

For the Household of Faith

Romans 15:5–7	Philippians 1:9–11	1 Thessalonians
Romans 15:13	Colossians 1:9–12	5:23–24
Ephesians 1:15–23	1 Thessalonians	2 Thessalonians
Ephesians 3:14–21	3:11–13	1:11–12

For the Advancement of Christ's Kingdom

Psalm 67:4	2 Corinthians	1 Thessalonians
Isaiah 61:11	2:14–16	2:4–12
Malachi 1:11	2 Corinthians 3:4–6	2 Thessalonians
1 Corinthians	Galatians 6:14	3:1–5
9:22–23	Ephesians 6:19–20	2 Timothy 4:1–2
1 Corinthians 15:58	Colossians 4:2–4	Philemon 6

For Loved Ones

Romans 12:9–13	Galatians 5:13–14	Titus 3:14
Romans 15:1–2	Galatians 5:22–24	Hebrews 10:24–25
Romans 15:5–7	Ephesians 4:1–3	James 2:1
1 Corinthians 1:10	Ephesians 4:31–32	James 3:17–18
1 Corinthians 4:5	Philippians 2:3–4	1 Peter 1:22
1 Corinthians 10:24	Colossians 3:12–17	1 Peter 3:8
1 Corinthians	1 Thessalonians	1 Peter 4:8–10
12:26–27	5:14–15	1 John 4:7, 11
1 Corinthians 13:4–8	2 Thessalonians 3:5	

THE GOSPEL IN YOUR
OWN WORDS

Here is an example of what it might look like to write the gospel in your own words.

God created humankind for his glory, happy and holy with souls that would never die. We rebelled against his authority, believing the lie of Satan that we could be, and would find pleasure in being, autonomous. With all of humankind, I became enslaved to the pursuit of self-advancement, doomed forever to live away from God's presence and peace and under his righteous judgment and wrath.

But God loved me. Not because I was lovable. But because he is love. He saved me. Not because of any righteousness in me, but out of the overflow of his grace and mercy. He poured out my deserved punishment on Jesus when, as a sinless substitute, he died in my place. God's justice was completely satisfied. God has clothed me in Christ's righteousness. God made me a welcomed and beloved member of his family.

God opened my heart to see the beauty of Jesus. Jesus, though fully divine, became a man, identifying with human weakness and vulnerabilities, maturing through obedience, prayer and the help of the Holy Spirit, and living the righteous life I never could. He is able to sympathize with my frailties and represent me before the father. He is the answer to all my needs. No one teaches like he does with authority, wisdom, and kindness. No one else can forgive me of my sin, wash me clean, and intercede for me. No one reigns like he does, protecting, leading ruling, overseeing, and subduing all evil.

God gave me faith to believe his promises are true. He made me willing and able to follow hard after him—to love him supremely and love people sacrificially. He has filled me with the hope of an eternity of loving and enjoying Him forever. He has given me his Spirit as a pledge of my inheritance in heaven.

God is finishing the work he has begun in me. I am who I am by God's gracious and wise design. My strengths are gifts for a fruitful service to him. My weaknesses he allows to keep me tethered close to him. God cares for me, desires my best, works for me. Not because I serve him perfectly, but because he loves me and by that love I will one day be: Holy. Blameless. Without spot or wrinkle.

SCRIPTURE-BASED PRAYERS FOR LOVED ONES

May he not be content to see in part, but may he seek you until he sees clearly. (Mark 8:22–25)

May she stand by the roads and ask for the ancient paths, where the good way is, and walk in it and find rest for her soul. (Jer. 6:16)

May he know the hope of his calling, the riches of the glory of his inheritance, and the greatness of your power. (Eph. 1:16–21)

May she see that all that is in the world is passing away, that it is nothing but a pleasure for the moment, that the end of it is vanity and grasping for the wind. (1 John 2:15–17; Heb. 11:24–26; Eccles. 2:1–3, 10–11)

May she discern the deceitfulness of charm and the vanity of beauty. Cause her to fear you, Lord. May she rejoice in the fruit of her hands. (Prov. 31:30–31)

Let him know the rewards of diligence in physical labor so that he may apply himself diligently to spiritual labors of virtue, knowledge, self-control, perseverance, godliness, brotherly kindness, and love. (1 Cor. 9:24–25; 2 Pet. 1:5–11)

May she know the deep satisfying joy of following you, being with you and being honored by you. (John 12:26)

May his boast be in you alone. (Jer. 9:23–24)

May he know that you can do all things and that no purpose of yours can be thwarted. May he not only hear of these things but also see them and see you. (Job 42:2, 5)

May her speech be honorable, good, beautiful, and fitting. May she know how to restrain her lips. (Prov. 10:19, 32)

May he desire wisdom and understanding more than gold or silver. (Prov. 3:13–16)

May he walk with uprightness knowing that you see all. May he wholeheartedly fear you. (Eccles. 12:13–14)

May she realize the importance of being faithful in little things and the impossibility of serving two masters. (Luke 16:10–13)

May he be careful how he walks, not as unwise but as wise, making best use of the time because the days are evil. May he not be foolish but understand what the will of the Lord is. (Eph. 5:15–17)

May her friendships be sharpening and stimulating. (Prov. 27:17; Heb. 10:24)

May he know that it is a very small thing to be judged by man. (1 Cor. 4:3)

Instruct and teach her in the way she should go. Let your steadfast love surround her and cause her to rejoice in you. (Ps. 32:8–11)

May he be a blameless child of God in the midst of a crooked and twisted generation. May he shine as a light in the world. May he hold fast to the word of life so that he will not run in vain. (Phil. 2:15–16)

SCRIPTURE-BASED PRAYERS FOR LOVED ONES

GOSPEL

PROMISES

PRAYERS

PROVISIONS

RESOURCES

May he acknowledge you in all his plans, trusting in you and not leaning on his own understanding. Make his paths straight. (Prov. 3:5–6)

May your word be a lamp to her feet and a light to her path. (Ps. 119:105)

Help him find enjoyment in his work because it pleases you. (Eccles. 2:24–26)

May she embrace an identity as a sojourner and exile, warring against and abstaining from fleshly passions. May her conduct be honorable and cause others to glorify you. (1 Pet. 2:11–12)

May he worship you by doing justice, loving kindness, and walking humbly before you. (Mic. 6:8)

May she fear you and delight in your commands. Give her both riches and righteousness so that she can stand on her own and stand clean before you. (Psalm 112)

Give her a patient heart that lives for eternity—waiting for the precious fruit of her labors, rejoicing in the early and late rains. (James 5:7–11)

May he find in you the satisfaction for his longing soul. (Psalm 107:9)

Give her a tender heart and a humble mind. (1 Pet. 3:8)

As he is confronted with evil people and imposters who are deceived and who deceive others, cause him to continue in what he has learned. May his acquaintance with Scripture grow deeper so that he becomes a man of God competent, and equipped for every good work. (2 Tim. 3:13–17)

Help him, by your grace, to behave in the world with simplicity and godly sincerity, not with earthly wisdom. (2 Cor. 1:12)

May she run with endurance the race you have set before her. May she be encouraged by the godly examples of others around her. May she keep her eyes on you. Help her to see and rid herself of distractions and burdens that keep her from running well. (Heb. 12:1–4)

Give her godly grief that produces repentance. (Luke 22:62; 2 Cor. 7:10)

May her aim be to please you and not live for herself. (2 Cor. 5:9, 15)

May he be like a man of Issachar who understands the times and will know what needs to be done. (1 Chron. 12:32)

May his wisdom be from above: pure, peaceable, gentle, open to reason, full of mercy and good fruits, impartial, and sincere. May he sow peace and reap righteousness. (James 3:17–18)

May she be kind and tenderhearted— feeling the joys and struggles of others. May she forgive the wrongs of those who have sinned against her, appreciating your mercy on her. (Eph. 4:32)

May his all-encompassing passion be that his actions and words and attitudes showcase the worth of the gospel. (Phil. 1:27)

May she live and labor faithfully to hear you say, "Well done, good and faithful servant." (Matt. 25:21)

May she strive to help others to maturity. May she know your powerfully energizing work within. (Col. 1:28–29)

BORROWED PRAYERS

O you who are full of compassion, I commit and commend myself unto you, in whom I am, and live, and know. Be the goal of my pilgrimage, and my rest by the way. Let my soul take refuge from the crowding turmoil of worldly thoughts beneath the shadow of your wings; let my heart, this sea of restless waves, find peace in you, O God.

AUGUSTINE

We beg you, Lord, to help and defend us. Deliver the oppressed, pity the insignificant, raise the fallen, show yourself to the needy, heal the sick, bring back those of your people who have gone astray, feed the hungry, lift up the weak, take off the prisoners' chains. May every nation come to know that you alone are God, that Jesus Christ is your child, that we are your people, the sheep that you pasture.

CLEMENT OF ROME

Lord, I thank you that your love constrains me. I thank you that, in the great labyrinth of life, you wait not for my consent to lead me. I thank you that you lead me by a way which I know not, by a way which is above the level of my poor understanding.

GEORGE MATHESON

Pity those who are afflicted, and who shall pass this night in wakefulness and pain. Help the tempted. Give peace to the troubled in mind. Be you a Father to the fatherless, and a God of consolation to those who are desolate and oppressed. And give us all grace, that we may abound in charity one toward another; and do good unto all men, according to our Lord's example and commandment.

HENRY THORNTON

Most holy and most merciful God, the strength of the weak, the rest of the weary, the comfort of the sorrowful, the Savior of the sinful, and the refuge of your children in every time of need, hear us while we pray for your help in all the circumstances and experiences of our life. When our hearts are growing cold and dead, and we are losing our vision of your face, and living as if life had no spiritual reality, help us, O God.

JOHN HUNTER

We offer up again our souls and bodies to you, to be governed, not by our own will, but yours. O let it be ever the ease and joy of our hearts, to be under the conduct of your unerring wisdom, to follow your counsels, and to be ruled in all things by your holy will. And let us never distrust your abundant kindness and tender care over us; whatsoever it is you wouldst have us to do, or to suffer in this world.

JOHN WESLEY

Now, O my Father, remember how weak I am, and how many things this day brings to me, to bear and to do. I know not what an hour may bring forth; but you know. I give myself into your hands. I ask you to guide me. I pray you to spare me trial; but if I am tried, to keep me from falling.

HENRY WOTHERSPOON

Grant Lord, we ask you, that we may learn to have our hopes and fears, our joys and sorrows, all grounded on your holy word, that we may learn to love what you love, and to hate that which you hate.

WILLIAM WILBERFORCE

O you plenteous source of every good and perfect gift, shed abroad the cheering light of your sevenfold grace over our hearts. Yea, Spirit of love and gentleness, we most humbly implore your assistance. You know our faults, our failings, our necessities, the dullness of our understanding, the waywardness of our affections, the perverseness of our will. When, therefore, we neglect to practice what we know, visit us, we ask you, with your grace, enlighten our minds, rectify our desires, correct our wanderings, and pardon our omissions, so that by your guidance we may be preserved from making shipwreck of faith, and keep a good conscience, and may at length be landed safe in the haven of eternal rest; through Jesus Christ our Lord.

ANSELM

We appeal, O Lord, to your mercies, knowing them to be much more greater than our sins; and you came not to call the righteous but the sinners to repentance: to who you say, Come unto me all you that are over laden and diseased with the burden of sins, and I will ease you and refresh you. Yes, Lord, you are that God which wills not the death of a sinner, but rather that he should turn and live, which wishes all men to be saved and to come to the knowledge of your truth. Therefore, O Lord, we humbly ask you, not to withdraw your mercies from us, because of our sins, but rather, O Lord, lay upon us your saving health, that you may show yourself toward us to be a Savior: for what greater praise can there be to a Physician, than to heal the sick; neither can there be any greater glory to you being a Savior, than to save sinners.

HENRY SMITH

My Father, I have moments of deep unrest—moments when I know not what to ask by reason of the very excess of my wants. I have in these hours no words for you, no conscious prayers for you. My cry seems purely worldly; I want only the wings of a dove that I may flee away. . . . But you know what I ask, O my God. You know the name of that need which lies beneath my speechless groan. You know that, because I am made in your image, I can find rest only in what gives rest to you; therefore you have counted my unrest unto me for righteousness, and have called my groaning your Spirit's prayer.

GEORGE MATHESON

Lord, arouse us to a deep concern for all with whom we come in contact from day to day. Make us all missionaries at home or in the street, or in our workshop; wherever providence has cast our lot, may we there shine as lights in the world.

CHARLES SPURGEON

Loving Lord and heavenly Father, I offer up today all that I am, all that I have, all that I do, and all that I suffer, to be Yours today and Yours forever. Give me grace, Lord, to do all that I know of Your holy will. Purify my heart, sanctify my thinking, correct my desires. Teach me, in all of today's work and trouble and joy, to respond with honest praise, simple trust, and instant obedience, that my life may be in truth a living sacrifice, by the power of Your Holy Spirit and in the name of Your Son Jesus Christ, my Master and my all. Amen.

ELISABETH ELLIOT

Lord, I do not know what to ask. You alone know what I need. You love me better than I know how to love myself. Oh Father! Give to your child what she herself is too ignorant to pray for. I dare not ask either for crosses or consolations. Simply present myself before you. I open my heart to you. I adore your purposes even though I don't know them. I am silent. I offer myself in sacrifice. I yield myself to you. I want to have no other desire than to accomplish your will. Teach me to pray. Pray yourself in me. Amen.

FRANCOIS DE LA MOTHE FENEOLON (TRANSLATED BY E.ELLIOT)

A FINAL WORD OF ENCOURAGEMENT

Though prayer is a pouring out of your heart before God, it is also a spiritual discipline that requires effort. Helplessness may motivate us to pray. Humility may teach us to pray. Discipline will keep us praying. Hopefully this journal will be a tool for developing a lifelong pattern of pouring out your heart to the Lord. Please remember, using this journal is meant to unburden your heart, not add a burdensome duty. I have learned there are seasons in a life of prayer and that praying uses mental and emotional "muscles" that take a while to develop. Praying out loud with a trusted friend has helped me learn to pray. Even still, very rarely do I pray completely through my whole journal.

My goal is to daily

- Read the Daily Gospel Truth
- Read through one section of the Promises (mark my place)
- Pray for one section in Kingdom Prayers (mark my place)
- Pray for one person in Loved Ones (mark my place)
- Pray for myself (mark my place)

Often in my prayer times I may

- Only read through the Daily Gospel Truths
- Only read the promises I am needing at the moment
- Only pray for the person the Lord has placed on my heart

Some of my yearly rhythms

- At every child's birthday/anniversary I write out a Scripture prayer for them
- Between Christmas and New Year's I record the provisions of God in the past year
- After I finish a Bible study I write out a prayer to apply what I have learned
- Whenever I find myself in a difficult situation, I search God's Word for a promise to hold onto.

I love it when I am able to settle into my chair in the mornings and open my journal. I will sigh contentedly. "Here I am, once again Lord, needing to have you set my heart and mind straight." Gospel truth steadies my heart and clears my vision. The promises of God recall to my mind God's loving kindness, power and faithfulness. Cheered by hope in his sovereign control over the future and amazed that he has allowed me to be part of his work on earth, I once again come dependent, submissive and expectant before the God of Creation and pour out my heart to him. He welcomes me into his presence with grace and peace.

Lois Krogh

Come my soul, thy suit prepare.
Jesus loves to answer prayer.
He Himself has bid thee pray,
Therefore will not say thee nay.
Thou art coming to a King.
Large petitions with thee bring.
For His grace and power are such,
None can ever ask too much.

JOHN NEWTON